Community Helpers

Helping Lead Activities

by Trudy Becker

FOCUS READERS

PIONEER

www.focusreaders.com

Focus Readers is distributed by North Star Editions:
sales@northstareditions.com | 888-417-0195

Produced for Focus Readers by Red Line Editorial.

Photographs ©: iStockphoto, cover, 1, 4, 7, 11, 18, 21; Shutterstock Images, 8, 12, 15, 17

Library of Congress Cataloging-in-Publication Data
Names: Becker, Trudy, author.
Title: Helping lead activities / Trudy Becker.
Description: Mendota Heights, MN : Focus Readers, 2024. | Series: Community helpers | Includes index. | Audience: Grades 2-3
Identifiers: LCCN 2023028126 (print) | LCCN 2023028127 (ebook) | ISBN 9798889980186 (hardcover) | ISBN 9798889980612 (paperback) | ISBN 9798889981459 (ebook pdf) | ISBN 9798889981046 (hosted ebook)
Subjects: LCSH: Community leadership--Juvenile literature. | Leadership--Juvenile literature.
Classification: LCC HM781 .B43 2024 (print) | LCC HM781 (ebook) | DDC 303.3/4--dc23/eng/20230724
LC record available at https://lccn.loc.gov/2023028126
LC ebook record available at https://lccn.loc.gov/2023028127

Printed in the United States of America
Mankato, MN
012024

About the Author

Trudy Becker lives in Minneapolis, Minnesota. She likes exploring new places and loves anything involving books.

Table of Contents

Chapter 1

Help from a Leader

A few girls sit around a table. They hold beads and string in their hands. An adult is there, too. She helps the girls make necklaces.

The adult is a **volunteer**. She leads a Girl Scout troop. She helps them with different **activities**. The woman is not paid. She does it to help her **community**.

Did You Know?

There are more than two million Girl Scout members. The same is true for Boy Scouts.

Chapter 2

Leading Activities

People enjoy doing things outside of school and work. Different activities can be fun. They can help people learn. And they can help people be **social**.

Some people help lead activities. Then others can join in. Leaders might hold **one-time** events. Or they might form groups that meet often. The leaders help make the plans.

Did You Know?

Going to see games or shows could be one-time events.

Chapter 3

Around Town

There are many kinds of group activities. Leaders might start book clubs. People can talk together about what they read. Leaders might start art groups. People can share their work.

Some places have community gardens. Leaders can plan activities for them. They can set up times for people to weed the gardens. They can also plan sales. People can sell what they grow.

Did You Know?

Some community groups make art together. They might paint walls in their towns.

Butterfly

THAT'S AMAZING!

Protest Leaders

Sometimes, people don't agree with laws. They want to change things. So, they express their ideas. They might **protest**. That can happen without plans and leaders. But often, leaders help. They can show people what to do.

TOGETHER
WE CAN
CHANGE

Chapter 4

Fundraisers

Fundraisers are useful for many groups. A group might need money to help someone. Or a group might need money for a new project. Leaders can help plan fundraisers.

Bake sales are a popular kind of fundraiser. People make different desserts. Then they sell them. The money helps support their groups. Then the groups can do their activities.

Did You Know?

Leaders often have helpers. That way, one person does not do all the work.

Bake Sale
Today

FOCUS ON

Helping Lead Activities

Write your answers on a separate piece of paper.

1. Write a sentence that explains one kind of activity that volunteers could help lead.
2. If you had to lead a community activity, what would you choose? Why?
3. What is one example of a fundraiser?
   A. a Girl Scout troop
   B. a bake sale
   C. a community garden
4. How could being social help people?
   A. People won't be as lonely.
   B. People can make more art.
   C. Social events make people tired.

Answer key on page 24.

Glossary

activities
Things that people can do.

community
A group of people and the places where they spend time.

fundraisers
Events to raise money for something.

one-time
Happening only once.

protest
To speak out and show that you disagree with something.

social
Being around other people.

volunteer
A person who helps without being paid.

To Learn More

BOOKS

Bassier, Emma. *Schools*. Minneapolis: Abdo Publishing, 2020.

Schell, Lily. *Community Center*. Minneapolis: Bellwether Media, 2023.

NOTE TO EDUCATORS

Visit **www.focusreaders.com** to find lesson plans, activities, links, and other resources related to this title.

Index

Answer Key: 1. Answers will vary; **2.** Answers will vary; **3.** B; **4.** A